ADD DIRT

AND

STIR

EXPERIMENTS WITH WHISKY AND GARDENING

By L. A. Sommerfeld

Add Dirt and Stir book has saved the following resources using 100% post-consumer recycled paper, printed with vegetable based inks using New Environmental Technology by **Seedsgreenprinting.com**

400 lbs wood preserved for the future	**1,631 gal** wastewater flow saved	**180 lbs** solid waste not generated	**355 lbs** net greenhouse gases prevented	**2,720,000 BTUs** energy not consumed

Review your reusing and recycling practices and invest in our future!

Cover photograph by Adam Milliron

For Jeslie,
Keep Growing!

THIS BOOK IS DEDICATED TO MY SON ELIOT
AND TO THE YAMPA VALLEY—THE VERY
REASONS MY HEART BEATS.

♥

I SUGGEST THAT YOU FIRST READ THE COCKTAIL RECIPE SECTION. YOU MAY WANT AN ENJOYABLY STIFF DRINK TO GET THROUGH THE OTHER PARTS OF THIS BOOK. MAKING SENSE OF SUCH DIVERGENT YET TOTALLY RELATED TOPICS REQUIRES THE SUPPORT OF A DRINK IN HAND. ☞

TABLE OF CONTENTS

TABLE OF CONTENTS

PREMISE: A GREAT COCKTAIL STARTS IN THE DIRT

Add Dirt and Stir was written as a grow-your-own guide for cocktail gardens. It also strives to cover some higher ground. I have made a brazen attempt to explain how to get real flavor in what you grow so that you can make a very tasty cocktail. It is my belief that a great cocktail starts in the dirt. The best way to make a fabulous cocktail is to use superb ingredients, and good dirt makes for superb ingredients.

This book is my way of encouraging all levels of enthusiasts to grow and create wonderful flavors in the garden. As one who finds the evening cocktail an indispensable luxury that likely keeps civilization simultaneously crazed and contained, I have given some thought to where it all comes from. There is an interconnectedness that exists among plants, animals, humans, and dirt, and I believe that if we mess with that we do so at our own peril.

This narrative is by no means an exhaustive treatment of such matters. If anything, it's the opposite. This book is a passionate curiosity pursued with an open mind—another road traveled.

I have sacrificed a portion of my sanity trying to include lots of gory details about soil and plant health. You may be surprised to learn how alike plants and people really are. All have varying levels of intensity and aroma. Depending on how much attention you pay to your dirt, seeds, and water, you can grow some great smelling and great tasting delicacies. Let's face it: just because something is good for you is often not inspiration enough. If it tastes good in a drink, however, that's a horse of another color. Crack on!

There is a later section in the book devoted to unique and flavorful cocktails. These are recipes that use some outstandingly smooth whisky from Virginia and herbs and flowers grown with *biological intention*. I realize that the term biological intention may sound a bit trendy, but there is real merit in this growing methodology. There are many challenges of process and progress facing modern agriculture. Corporate farms are dominating the world's food supply. Now, that may not mean much to you if you are someone who looks no further for sustenance than a fast-food counter or meat and produce kept fresh under cling wrap in supermarket displays. But if you have even half a non-genetically-modified cell left in your body, then you can see that *corporate* and *farm* are two words that should never come together to name a place where plants and animals are raised for food.

There is a lot of discussion these days about genetic modification of plants and animals, and I do address the topic. It's important to remember, however, that genetic modification is only one of the ways that food is contaminated, adulterated, and made less nutritious today. I believe at least part of the problem with our food is that we have entered an era in which corporate bullies rather than farmers are growing what we eat. When food is a commodity whose purpose is to bolster corporate earnings, the game becomes how to produce it as cheaply as possible. Quality is relatively unimportant. In the world of corporate food production, quality can't hold a candle to cost.

Corporate agriculture is putting the human community itself at risk. We are consuming stressed and sick plants and animals. That's not good for the plants and animals, and it's not good for us. How does food like that enable people to be at their best? How does it even allow for survival?

I believe that small, local, intelligent agricultural movements are imperative to the health of our bodies and the health of our communities. By growing more of our own food, we reestablish that primal bond between human beings and the dirt that sustains life. Growing our own food creates the conscious space for pride to coexist with humility and gratitude. It grounds the human being. This is just my opinion, but with all the electromagnetic residue we're inflicting on ourselves via our technological advancement, I think the human race could stand to ground ourselves for a damn good while. Perhaps as we provide better, more natural food for proper nutrition, the result will ultimately be a community populated by healthier, kinder, more capable, open hearted, and connected human beings.

Increasing numbers of men and women are going into organic farming and traditional food and drink preparation. The ones closest to my heart are those who are pioneering the frontiers of distilling in America. To that, I say Amen! We can all use a well-crafted, locally produced drink during or after the evening news these days.

The rapidly growing segment of small-craft distillers is paralleling the success of microbreweries a decade ago. At the time of this writing, there are over 200 licensed craft distilleries in the U.S. Not since Prohibition have spirits enjoyed such devoted attention and creative manipulation.

I have highlighted the products of Copper Fox Distillery from Sperryville, Virginia in my recipes for many reasons. A few years ago I owned a wine and spirits import business and discovered Wasmund's Copper Fox Distillery through a friend who recommended it to me. The magic that makes Wasmund's what it is lies somewhere between crude science and cosmic magnetic impulse. I am a self-admitted, unabashed evangelist for the stuff! It's noteworthy when you stumble upon something that leaves you better for finding it. Wasmund's whisky does that. I can drink other whisky, but it never seems to deliver the magic of Copper Fox. As luck would have it, I found inspiration at the bottom of a bottle of Single Malt, and you're holding the result of that magical spark.

Add Dirt and Stir will hopefully leave you curious about the beginnings, middles, and endings of a cocktail, a garden, a grower, a government, and you. I hope it will also leave you with a new respect for dirt. Enjoy!

PART 1

Creating a
Cocktail Garden

Growing Flavor

Life is way too short and often complicated to drink cheap liquor and to eat food with lackluster flavor.

I can taste and smell the difference that foliar feeding, proper soil amendments, and good seeds make in the quality of my botanicals. When I put a sprig of lovingly cultivated Kentucky Colonel mint and a Tagetes marigold blossom in with my single malt, the herbs speak for themselves. Do a comparison test. Make the same drink with just-harvested, homegrown herbs and with overpriced, supermarket herbs that were probably harvested weeks ago. I have found the menthol component of homegrown mints to be far superior. You get AROMA! and taste. I chose the recipes in this book as much for the smell they produce as for their taste. Paying attention to your soil and applying foliar feedings are a major plus for growing beautifully aromatic as well as flavorful herbs and vegetables.

You experience four taste sensations on your tongue: sweet, salt, bitter, and sour. (Some people say there are five—the fifth being umami or savory taste.) Complexity in flavor comes through your olfactory sensors. Most of your taste sensation is actually a function of what you smell. It is challenging to SAY what you smell and taste. Try it. Close your eyes and try to identify smells and tastes without seeing what you are sensing. You will find your vocabulary suddenly limited. With practice, however, you can develop a high level of acumen within your sense of smell. With a better nose, your experience with food and flavor will be taken to a quantum—even tantric—dimension.

You might be surprised to discern a difference in the flavor intensity between commercially grown, store bought, and homegrown. Trust me—there is indeed a big difference. Just because something is homegrown, however, does not mean it has superior flavor. Homegrown food will no doubt have a fresher taste, but complexity may still be lacking. In order to achieve complexity in flavor, you need to pay attention to the geekier side of gardening.

The good news is that herbs are some of the easiest things to grow. The bad news is that you still need to do some work. You can't just throw a seed in the dirt and wake up the next morning to find a magic beanstalk growing outside your window.

To end up with a fabulous cocktail, you have to start with flavorful herbs and vegetables. For ingredients with flavor, you need to pay attention to five important principles:

1. Plant the right plant in the right place
2. Provide good dirt for your plants
3. Give your plants enough water but not too much
4. Pay attention to seed DNA
5. Give your plants proper attention

I discuss each of the first four principles in the next four sections. Tips regarding the last point—giving proper attention to your plants—are scattered throughout the gardening part of this book.

TIP: IT IS A GOOD IDEA TO KEEP IN MIND SPACING AND HEIGHT REQUIREMENTS. LETTUCES AND OTHER GREENS PREFER BEING IN DIRECT SUN ONLY PART OF THE DAY, AND THEY PREFER MODERATE MOISTURE IN THE SOIL. I RECOMMEND GROWING SOME TALLER PLANTS AROUND LETTUCES TO HELP CREATE SHADE AND RETAIN MOISTURE. BORAGE IS GREAT FOR THIS, AS ARE TOMATOES, BUT THEY DO GET BIG. THIS YEAR I LET THINGS GET A LITTLE MESSY IN MY GARDEN JUST TO SEE HOW THINGS WOULD WORK OUT. TURNS OUT THAT SOME PLANT DENSITY ALLOWED HEIRLOOM LETTUCES TO LAST LONGER DESPITE OPPRESSIVE HEAT AND DROUGHT.

PLANNING YOUR GARDEN:
PLANT THE RIGHT PLANT IN THE RIGHT PLACE

Gardens can be a welcome reprieve from the onslaught of technology, temptation, and banality. A garden can be one pot or an acre or more. It's less about its breadth than its content. Below, I have broken down into a sketch-type format how to approach your cocktail garden. The same criteria apply to any size garden.

Gardening is a constant. A little here and a little there is probably a good approach to take. Trying to tackle everything the first year will make you put your head in your hands and cause your eyes to spout water. There is more to know about gardening than time left on the planet, so just accept it.

With a cocktail in hand, make a plan for the garden you want to create. Keep in mind what your purpose is and what the plants need, and then create a suitable space. There are a few basic things to consider that can help demystify the process:

1. The right plant in the right **PLACE** or condition equals success. Bananas don't grow in Alaska. Climate is a big factor in what you can grow. Make sure the plants you want to grow will grow in the part of the world where you live. The USDA Plant Hardiness Zone Map is a useful tool to help you figure out which plants will flourish in your garden.

2. Determine how much **SPACE** you have—a large plot, roomy containers, a raised bed, or a small pot on a windowsill—to determine which varieties you will grow. If all you have is a windowsill and you want to grow basil, you'll want to choose a dwarf variety and not one that can grow to six feet tall.

3. How much **LIGHT** does your space receive? Does it receive direct sun all day or is it always in shade? When does the direct sunlight start and when does it end? You'll need to choose plants that do well in those lighting conditions.

4. What kind of **DIRT** do you have? Where you are growing will be a factor in what you grow and what medium you use for soil. If you're creating a garden in a plot of land, find out what type of soil you have—sand, clay, silt, or loam. You also have to look into what your selected cultivars need to thrive. Some need sandy, dry soil conditions. Most prefer well-drained soils.

5. What's the **PURPOSE** of your garden? Are you growing plants for decorative use, culinary use, or both?

> TIP: I RECOMMEND PLANTING ANYTHING YOU WANT TO HARVEST REGULARLY IN AN EASY-TO-ACCESS AREA OF THE BED. IT'S A PAIN TO HAVE TO REACH AROUND NON-ESSENTIAL PLANTS CONSTANTLY TO GET TO THE PLANTS YOU NEED EVERY DAY.

SAMPLE GARDEN PLAN

HERE IS AN EXAMPLE OF A GARDEN PLAN:
PURPOSE: DECORATIVE AND CULINARY
SPACE: SMALL OUTDOOR PATIO
LIGHT: FULL SUN ALL DAY

RECOMMENDATIONS:

*   FOR THIS SPACE, CONTAINERS OR A RAISED BED WOULD BE GOOD.
*   THE DIRT SHOULD BE A MIXTURE OF LEAF MULCH, QUALITY COMPOST, AND SCREENED TOPSOIL.

Once you have put together this information sketch, determine which plants best fit your conditions and purpose. (See the Cultivar List on page 64 for some options for a cocktail garden.)

Provide Good Dirt for Your Plants

What Is Dirt?

Dirt is the medium in which most plants live. As such, it is the source of the food for most life on Earth. The main components of dirt are minerals, decomposed animal and plant matter, microorganisms such as bacteria and fungi, water, air, and earth energy.

As far as plants are concerned, the most important area of the soil is the **rhizosphere**, which encompasses the top four to five inches below the soil surface and is the most biologically active part of the soil. It is in this area, immediately adjacent to plants' roots, that plants obtain most of their nutrients and the ability to suppress disease. Just how biologically active is the rhizosphere in a healthy plot of soil? It boggles the mind. This top few inches of healthy soil is teeming with millions upon millions of microorganisms—including mycorrhizal species, fungi, and bacteria—all practicing a form of mutualism that enables root systems to develop and sustains plant growth. Mutualism is the relationship between two organisms of **different** species that biologically interact in a way that each individual benefits. Interestingly enough, this same principle when it occurs between two individuals of the **same** species is called... wait for it... cooperation. At its best, dirt is alive with relationships that would put most human interaction to shame.

The proliferation of chemical herbicides and pesticides has had a devastating effect on soil quality. The widespread use of toxic chemicals devastates micronutrient populations in the soil, affecting crop growth. In areas where herbicides and pesticides have been widely used, topsoil erosion has become epidemic as the soil surface forms a hard crust and rainwater just washes off the top, never penetrating the earth. Essentially, the dirt has become dead. There are no microbial populations of fungi and bacteria to break the minerals down for plants to consume. Dirt that was once rich with life has become a barren wasteland.

Dr. Elaine Ingham, a soil biology researcher and Chief Scientist at the Rodale Institute, explains, "It's very necessary to have these organisms. They will supply your plant with precisely the right balances of all the nutrients as the plant requires. When you start to realize that one of the major roles and functions of life in the soil is to provide nutrients to the plants in the proper forms, then we don't need inorganic fertilizers. We certainly don't have to have genetically engineered plants or to utilize inorganic fertilizers if we get this proper biology back in the soil."[1]

If you're wise, you'll take the time to understand and support the community of life that makes up the dirt in your garden. That way, you'll include yourself in the relationship of mutualism in your garden. By making sure the organisms that support your plants are at their best, your plants will benefit and so will you.

Erosion claims 24 billion tons of topsoil from the world's agricultural land every year. Scientists estimate that it takes nature 100 to 500 years to create one inch of topsoil.

There are three things in particular you can do to provide good dirt for your plants and ensure that it's teeming with microbial life: know the pH of your soil, use organic soil amendments, and inoculate the soil.

Give Your Plants Proper Attention: Know Your pH

An important aspect of soil health is its pH—a measurement of its acidity or alkalinity. You need to know your garden soil's pH. Different plants have different pH requisites. Many plants thrive in a slightly acidic to neutral soil, but others need greater acidity or alkalinity. This may seem overly technical, but planting good-quality seeds or plants in soil with less than ideal pH is going to work against your efforts. You can purchase a pH meter through Pike Agri-Lab Supplies and most garden supply stores. (See Guide to Resources.)

International Ag Labs advises that ideal soil pH should be 6.4 or thereabouts. When pH is correct, nutrients are more bioavailable. That's as important for plants as it is for people.

The soil's pH determines the chemical forms of its nutrients and thus affects plants' ability to take up those nutrients. If the pH of the soil is not right for a plant (if it moves too far one way or the other from the ideal pH), certain nutrients get "bound up" (which to me sounds similar to constipation in humans). When that happens, the plant's root system cannot access enough essential nutrients in the proper forms of minerals and enzymes, resulting in dysbiosis, a condition that affects enzymatic and microbial balance. When there are imbalances, there are symptoms of it. A plant that cannot access useable nutrients will become unhealthy, and an unhealthy plant will exhibit symptoms of distress. It may still grow and even reproduce and bear fruit, but it will probably not be flavorful or abundant. We are talking about a difference that happens on the molecular level.

Learn to notice the symptoms of imbalance, which can include yellowing leaves, curling leaf tips, wilting, red spots on the leaves, deformed fruit, stunted growth, and excessive vigor.

PH SCALE

Acidic 4.5–5.5	Neutral 6.6–7.3
Moderately Acidic 5.6–6.2	Moderately Alkaline 7.4–8.4
Ideal 6.3–6.5	Alkaline 8.5 +

Give Your Plants Proper Attention: Use Organic Soil Amendments

Colorado State University Extension defines a soil amendment as "any material added to a soil to improve its physical properties, such as water retention, permeability, water infiltration, drainage, aeration and structure" so as to create a better environment for plants' roots.[2] Check your soil's pH and know your soil type before adding soil amendments. You need to figure out where you are before you can determine how to get to where you want to be.

There are dozens of types of soil amendments. Check your state agricultural extension resources for examples of the amendments to use in your garden and how best to apply them. I prefer to use organic amendments. According to a fact sheet from Colorado State University Extension, organic amendments improve soil conditions in various ways: "Organic amendments increase soil organic matter content and offer many benefits. Over time, organic matter improves soil aeration, water infiltration, and both water- and nutrient-holding capacity. Many organic amendments contain plant nutrients and act as organic fertilizers. Organic matter also is an important energy source for bacteria, fungi and earthworms that live in the soil."[3] Improved soil conditions enable plants to fend off disease and insect pressure without the need for pesticides.

Give Your Plants Proper Attention: Inoculate the Dirt

Whether you start your garden from seed or buy plants, it's important to inoculate the soil prior to planting. Inoculation is the addition of bacteria or fungi generally in powdered form to the soil. Inoculating the soil is critical to help establish adequate populations of microorganisms that will benefit the root systems of your plants. One product that I highly recommend is **Jubilate** from International Ag Labs. Jubilate is a broad-spectrum microbial inoculant in powder form that helps the plant's root system get established by being the Welcome Wagon for surrounding microorganisms in the dirt. Who doesn't love a new neighbor to stop in with a fresh baked pie and a bottle of Wasmund's? You most definitely want a microbial party in your soil—the more the merrier—and an inoculant is an easy way to get the party started. The scientific significance of inoculating the soil is that the microbes that are unleashed make nutrients available to the plant roots, chelate them properly, and transfer the nutrients up into the plants. That is a gross oversimplification of an amazing and complex process.

WATER YOUR PLANTS ENOUGH BUT NOT TOO MUCH

There are a few basic principles for watering plants successfully. Most importantly, do not use chlorinated water for plants. Rainwater is best. In general, water when the top two to four inches of soil is dry. Thorough watering is more useful than frequent watering. More plants than boaters are killed by drowning.

It is a good idea to group your plants and flowers by how much water they need. Plant those that like it drier in one area, and those that prefer moisture in another.

Below I discuss three ways to give proper attention to your plants that have to do with watering. The first is foliar feeding, which means giving additional nutrition to your plants while you water them. The other two points—mulching and paying attention to drainage—have to do with ensuring that your plants receive the right amount of moisture.

Give Your Plants Proper Attention: Foliar Feeding

In addition to watering the soil, it's a good idea to invest in a pump sprayer and **foliar feed**. This method is very beneficial in providing essential nutrients to the leaf surfaces of plants. You add liquid amendments to the water in the sprayer and spray above and below leaf surfaces. It is best to do foliar feeding at daybreak, well before the sunlight becomes intense. If you spray in direct light, you will scald your plants. (See the Guide to Resources. Both Advancing Eco Agriculture and International Ag Labs sell liquid forms of calcium, potassium, micronized sea minerals, and other essential nutrients to use in foliar application.) You will typically spray once a week.

16

The amendments you spray will change during the growing season. Follow application rate directions. More is not better in this instance.

Give Your Plants Proper Attention: Use Mulch

Skirt the base of your plants with a layer of straw or double-shredded wood chips to control weeds and help retain moisture. Mulching will help your plants grow better and will save you time and labor in your garden.

Give Your Plants Proper Attention: Pay Attention to Drainage

In addition to lots of sun and thorough watering, most herbs and flowering plants require well-drained soil. Nobody likes wet feet, at least not all the time.

Drainage is important because plant roots need oxygen. Without proper drainage, the soil becomes anaerobic and the roots will suffocate. To determine how compact your soil is—and therefore how good its drainage is—do this simple test: Grab a handful of damp dirt from a patch in your garden and close your fist around it. Ideally it should clump slightly while staying relatively loose. If the dirt forms a solid ball, it probably has too much clay. If it forms no clumps at all, it is probably too sandy. Either way, your garden may well have drainage issues.

To help create better drainage in clay soil, it is a good idea to add sand and soil amendments such as compost, sphagnum peat, or aged manure. For better drainage in sandy soil, add soil amendments such as greensand, kelp meal, or an organic fertilizer blend and be sure to add mulch to retain moisture. If you are planting in a pot or bed, you can help ensure decent drainage by lining the bottom with small stones or gravel and then adding well-mixed soil.

Pay Attention to Seed DNA

"Wondering is the seed of genius."
William Mocca

Why does seed DNA matter? In a culinary or cocktail garden, seed DNA is the critical component in the plant's potential to express great flavor. It comes down to taste versus yield. There is debate about this, but in general vigorous growth and large yields may be obtained at the expense of complexity in flavor. For the purpose of backyard cocktail gardeners growing the most flavorful ingredients, seed type will play a large role. Let's look at some differences among the types of seeds you are likely to come by: heirloom, open pollinated, hybrid, and genetically modified.

An **heirloom seed** is from a plant that has been grown, saved, and carefully passed from one generation to another because its flavor, productivity, hardiness, or adaptability is considered valuable. Many heirloom varieties have been passed down for more than a hundred years. These plants often have the best flavor and do well in small gardens.

An **open-pollinated seed** (OP) is a variety that can be harvested from the plant, saved, and replanted and the same plant variety will regrow the next year. All heirloom seeds are open pollinated, but not all open-pollinated seeds are heirlooms. The newer varieties are not old enough to be considered heirlooms. Open-pollinated seeds have modest vigor and yields, but are noted for producing plants with great flavor. Propagation is by wind, insects, animals, or itself.

A **hybrid seed** is produced by artificially cross-pollinating two genetically different plants of the same species, such as two different tomatoes. The cross-pollination is done by hand, and a seed that is saved will not grow true to either parent. Hybrids are typically bred for commercial use. They have higher yields, more uniformity, and greater disease resistance. Hybridization does not mean genetic modification.

Aside from flavor, the most notable difference between plants grown from open-pollinated seeds and hybrids is vigor. Charles Darwin described the phenomenon of *hybrid vigor* in the 1870s. John Navazio, the Senior Scientist for the Organic Seed Alliance, explains that the advantages of hybrid vigor can be particularly valuable to gardeners in extreme climates: "The seeds emerge more vigorously and uniformly. They are stronger and the plants perform better under a wide range of adverse climate conditions."[4]

That does not necessarily mean that hybrid seeds are better than OPs. Which are the best seeds to plant? Ben Watson, in his article "Hybrid or Open Pollinated," writes this as the bottom line: "Perhaps the most useful answer comes from Rob Johnston [the founder and chairman of Johnny's Selected Seeds]. His advice is to look beyond labels: 'The consumer in me wants settled-down varieties,' he says, 'ones that might not have the power of the most vigorous hybrids but that grow well enough.... The best varieties have a certain vitality, which involves complex combinations of genes. Home gardeners, Johnston advises, should be open to growing any plant that looks interesting to them.'"[5]

The final type of seeds I want to discuss is **genetically modified** (GM). The DNA of these seeds has been altered using DNA from completely different species and organisms to give the plants traits that would be otherwise impossible. For example, genetically modified varieties of soy, corn, and canola are available in which a gene from a soil bacterium has been incorporated into the plant's DNA, which gives the plant the ability to tolerate the herbicide glyphosate. These seeds are marketed as Roundup Ready. That is just one example of how seeds are being genetically engineered. In my opinion, you should avoid GM seeds.

One of the arguments often used to promote genetic modification is that it is simply an extension of hybridization, and humans have been safely hybridizing plants and animals for centuries. But GM plants are not just high-tech hybrids. Here is how soil biology expert Dr. Elaine Ingham explains hybridization: "By definition, when we're doing normal genetic manipulation using breeding methods [hybridization], it's all going to be done within the normal, natural restrictions of reproductive abilities of organisms. You can't go outside the species."[6] Modern genetic engineering goes far beyond reproductive abilities that can occur in nature—blending genetic material not only from different species but also from different kingdoms of organisms.

Here are some examples. It is possible to create a hybrid of two different tomato plants. It is not possible, however, to create a hybrid of a tomato and a fish or of a corn plant and a bacterium. Blending the genetic material of two very different species from entirely different kingdoms of organisms is genetic modification. Fish and tomatoes can never mate and reproduce in nature. Neither can corn and bacteria. Some scientists fear that we are opening Pandora's box by creating food crops this way.

Whether you consider genetic modification a Pandora's box or the key to humanity's long-term survival, there is a simple yet practical reason to avoid using GM seeds in your garden. To put it simply, genetically modified plants tend to be less flavorful and nutritious than plants that are not genetically modified. The reason has to do with secondary metabolites, which do not develop to any significant degree in GM plants. Secondary metabolites are chemicals produced by plants that are important for the plants' survival but not (as far as scientists can tell) for any of the primary functions such as growth, photosynthesis, and reproduction. These compounds are believed to have protective value to the plants that produce them. As a by-product, they confer flavor and nutritive value to the plants that produce them. When extracted, secondary metabolites are used as medicines, flavorings, or recreational drugs. Some examples of secondary metabolites are caffeine, tetrahydrocannbinol (which is present in *Cannabis*), codeine, steroids, quercetin, and resveratrol. There are thousands of secondary metabolites, and many are being studied for their health benefits. Genetically modified plants never develop secondary metabolites to a degree where they actually have flavorful taste or provide quality nutrition.

YOU DON'T HAVE TO START YOUR GARDEN FROM SEED

IF YOU ARE A BEGINNER AND FEEL DAUNTED BY THE PROSPECT OF STARTING YOUR GARDEN FROM SEED, YOU MIGHT PREFER TO START WITH LIVE PLANTS. IF YOU DO, TRY THE GROWERS EXCHANGE. THEY HAVE AN ONLINE CATALOG OF FABULOUS STUFF. KEEP IN MIND THAT BUYING LIVE PLANTS IS PRICEY COMPARED TO BUYING SEEDS. IF YOU WOULD LIKE TO START YOUR PLANTS FROM SEED, HERE ARE TWO SOURCES I HIGHLY RECOMMEND: BOUNTIFUL GARDENS (A PROJECT OF ECOLOGY ACTION) AND PEACEFUL VALLEY FARM & GARDEN SUPPLY. (SEE GUIDE TO RESOURCES.)

GMO TIDBITS

If what I've written about genetically modified plants sounds as if I've sampled too many of my own recipes, consider just a few of the points from a special report from the Institute of Science in Society about GMOs and the glyphosate-based herbicides that are used extensively on genetically modified crops:

- "Livestock illnesses are linked to GM diets and include reproductive problems, diarrhea, bloating, spontaneous abortions, reduced live births, inflamed digestive systems, and nutrient deficiency."

- "There is a wealth of evidence on the health hazards of glyphosate. Its approval … relies on systematic flaws in the EU and US regulatory processes, which to this day, do not require evaluation by independent research, and instead rely solely on the industry's own studies…. Nevertheless, raw data have been obtained from the industry through the law courts, which, when re-analysed by independent scientists, also provide evidence of toxicity."

- "Taken together, glyphosate is implicated in *birth and reproductive defects, endocrine disruption, cancers, genotoxicity, neurotoxicity, respiratory problems, nausea, fever, allergies and skin problems.*"

- "Glyphosate-based herbicides are now the most commonly used herbicides in the world. It is still promoted as 'safe', despite damning evidence of serious harm to health and the environment."[7]

I warned you that you might want to make a stiff drink before starting to read this.

TIDBIT: In 1995, the Bt Potato was the first pesticide-producing plant approved by the EPA. This is a potato bred with genetic material from Bt bacteria, which generates a toxin that kills the Colorado Potato Beetle and other insects. Bt is a natural pesticide used safely by organic farmers when it is sprayed on plants, but it appears to produce far different consequences when it is introduced into the genetic material of plants. Dr. Elaine Ingham of the Rodale Institute explains that there is clear evidence of harm in animals that consume plants modified with genetic material from Bt bacteria, including "severe ulceration, starting in the digestive system" and "massive damage to the liver and to many of the internal organs."[8]

TIDBIT: Many GM plants are genetically engineered to resist the herbicide glyphosate, which is used in a number of herbicides including Roundup, Rodeo, and Pondmaster. Glyphosate was first patented in 1963 as a biocide. (The word biocide is derived from the Greek word for life and the Latin word for kill.) It was re-patented in 1974 as an herbicide, and has also been patented as an antibiotic. Glyphosates have a 22-year half-life, which means every application of this herbicide/biocide/antibiotic will lose only half its toxicity after 22 years. That's a mighty long time for a broad-spectrum weed killer to keep working.

TIDBIT: Glyphosate is the most popular herbicide in the world today. At least 880 million pounds are applied to crops worldwide every year.

Dr. Don Huber, professor emeritus of plant pathology at Perdue University, compares the toxicity of glyphosate to that of DDT. It is a cumulative chronic toxin. Even small amounts are toxic to humans:

- 0.5 parts per million (ppm) is toxic to the endocrine hormone system
- 1 ppm is toxic to the liver
- 10 ppm is cytotoxic to kidney cells[9]

In June 2013, the EPA ruled to allow a massive increase of the amount of glyphosate in food. Soybeans and flax, for example, may now contain as much as 40 ppm of glyphosate, double the previous allowable limit. The amount allowed in teff used for animal feed is now 100 ppm. In food crops such as potatoes, the allowable limits were raised from 200 ppm to 6,000 ppm.

TIDBIT: In a recent interview, Dr. Don Huber, one of the world's leading experts on genetically engineered plants, described how glyphosates differ from other herbicides: "We know that all herbicides are chelators, mineral chelators. That's how they compromise the plant's physiology: they tie up a particular nutrient and shut down a physiologic pathway.... But the thing that was different [with glyphosate] was its biocidal effect. It's not only a chelator, but it's also a strong antibiotic to beneficial microorganisms. How do you compensate for that? How do you restore biological activities?"[10]

PLANTS ARE LIKE PEOPLE

It is obvious to most people that humans have a lot in common with certain animals—apes in particular. It is not so obvious that we humans also share some significant traits with plants. Plants are like people. Really. Like people, plants require high-functioning digestive systems and quality macronutrients to be healthy. The health of both people and plants also includes a complex, symbiotic relationship with bacteria and other microorganisms. Also, let's not overlook the importance of love to the well being of both. And the following statement may solidify my place in the hall of kooks, but both humans and plants have a quantum existence. We are all energy. Your thoughts and intentions create energy, and plants absorb that energy. Who knows? The opposite may also be true.

The most important thing to take away here is that you want healthy, active dirt. It's important for your plants, and it's important for you. Healthy, active dirt will give your plants the opportunity to exhibit all their inherent genius or genus—however you choose to look at it. They will be naturally pest resistant, and there will be no need for you to use toxic chemicals, synthetic fertilizers, or excess water.

If you think of dirt as a digestive system, it is similar to an immune system. In the human body, over seventy percent of your immune system is located in your gut. When you consume plants that have strong immunity, you benefit by ingesting quality bioavailable nutrients and minerals into your own digestive system, which promotes the production of beneficial gut bacteria. This in turn improves enzymatic function and results in improved cell structure and immunity. When you have a high-functioning gut, you are undeniably healthier. A healthy gut helps reduce chronic inflammation, which is the single biggest catalyst for a wide range of diseases—from hay fever and periodontitis to atherosclerosis, many cancers, and arthritis. The list of benefits of a healthy gut is lengthy and substantial. The old saying You Are What You Eat is most assuredly true. The standard American diet with its dominant ingredients of refined sugars and genetically modified what nots is a case study in how poor nutrition contributes to disease.

There are three macronutrients: carbohydrates, proteins, and fats. People who consume complex carbohydrates, quality lean proteins, and a complex array of good-quality fats tend to be healthier, with better integrity of cell structure, a greater population of digestive enzymes, improved immune function, and increased and sustained energy compared to those who eat the standard American diet. In a striking parallel, plants that have quality photosynthesis and the resulting production of the same macronutrients show greater immunity to disease and insect pressure. That's another way that plants are like people. Like us, they are what they eat.

The best anti-aging tool out there is only a pot of dirt away. Grow and eat vegetables and herbs. If you eat better, you'll look better.

PART 2

Making a Great Cocktail

COCKTAIL HOUR

The cocktail hour is at hand! The recipes on the following pages are the results of experiments I conducted last summer. I spent many a fine day coming up with new cocktails. Sometimes the drink I created was a tasty treat. Those are the recipes that follow. Sometimes what I made was a mess. I did not include instructions for those. I even made myself sick more than once—not purposely, of course, but sometimes things zig when you thought they'd zag and then they make you gag. It's a small price to pay for innovation.

In these recipes, you will notice that ice is an important ingredient. I believe that ice should be given more attention as an ingredient in cocktails because it clearly affects flavor in a drink. After all, it provides additional water and surface area. The bases for the ice were variously infused with simple syrups, candy, or anything else that looked like fun and flavor. Make up your own versions to suit your taste preferences. These are merely sketches and, more importantly, a working example of what you can produce when you grow herbs with biological intention and use them in one of my favorite food groups—booze.

The word *whisky* comes from the Gaelic word *uisgebaugh* (wys-ger-baw), which means "water of life." Whisky is made from cereal grain. Its style and flavor are determined by where it is made, the types and proportions of grains that are used, the distillation method, and the aging process.

The grains used by Copper Fox are rye and barley. They are grown on stately lands in the northern neck of Virginia on Mantua Farm. According to family lore, Eleanor Roosevelt spent a weekend at the farm enjoying its splendor. Billy Dawson, farmer extraordinaire, lived on the farm for 18 years and still works these lands. He says, "If you stand here long enough, you'll take root."

As the wind blows, light hits the beards of the grain and they wave as a majestic green mass. Barley is an inviting sea. It is so optimistic, free, and kind with a graceful ease that makes you want to keep trying.

At Copper Fox, the barley is floor malted and raked every five hours. It is then put in the kiln and smoked with apple and cherry wood. From there it is made into a sumptuous mash and meets its ultimate glory in a 105-gallon pot still. Aging varies, but is seldom longer than 12 to 14 months in American oak. The depth of flavor that Copper Fox achieves generally requires much longer aging. Traditionally, whisky ages for years, not months. One of the many incredible innovations at Copper Fox has been to achieve balance, complexity, and smoothness in their whisky in less than two years.

EQUIPMENT AND OTHER ITEMS YOU WILL NEED

Muddler (also affectionately known as the Epiphany Stick)
(see note)

Glass measuring cups

Measuring spoons

Double jigger

Shaker

Strainer

Lewis bag

Stir

Blender
Ice sphere molds and ice trays (see note)
Cocktail glassware
A full array of herbs, fruits, and alcoholic ingredients

NOTE: How to Use a Muddler
When using the muddler or Epiphany Stick, muddle with liquid. Don't pulverize unless the recipe instructs you to. You want to bruise the ingredients to extract their essential oils.

How to Make Ice Spheres and Flavored Ice
Many of the recipes that follow call for ice spheres. These are pieces of ice made in a spherical mold. They can be solid or hollow. I use solid ice spheres in my recipes because they melt much slower than normal ice cubes. The ones in my recipes are intensely flavored. If you don't have an ice sphere mold, you can use a conventional ice cube tray to make the flavored-ice recipes. It's not a perfect substitute, but it will work. The basic recipe for making herb-infused simple syrup, which is the basis for flavored cocktail ice, can be found on page 61.

Let's catch our breath and recap here for a moment. What I hope to leave you with, in addition to great-tasting cocktail recipes, is an appreciation for the fact that the quality of what you eat and drink is greatly affected by how you produce it. In turn, the quality of the food you eat shows up in its flavor and its nutritional value. Higher quality food tends to be more flavorful and more nutritious. For better or for worse, the food you eat does affect your health. We are what we eat.

I wanted to write this book because I know that there are some people who will grasp this understanding more easily through a quality, handcrafted, stiff drink than through a plate of food. If you are one of those people, be aware that the importance of quality ingredients reaches far beyond mints and botanicals. Having quality ingredients for a cocktail is a great place to start, but it's essential to look at the bigger picture. Almost all food can be traced back to plants that grow in dirt. Either you eat those plants directly, or you eat the animals that ate the plants. To grow high-quality plants, you need to pay attention to seed source, the set up of your garden, and dirt quality and composition. To my way of thinking, it all comes down to the dirt. If you aren't interested in growing your own food, that's perfectly fine. But, for the love of man, please support—via the dollars you spend on what you eat—those folks who are farming with integrity. It is the dollar that will dictate play.

It is my opinion that greater attention should be given to the integrity of source and how corporate agriculture and Congress work against a healthy global society by funding substandard farming practices that produce food not fit for consumption by humans or animals. The habitual and obscene capitulation by those who govern to lobbies and corporate minions should not be tolerated by anyone who has the freedom to elect lawmakers. Industrialized agriculture has had a devastating effect on the integrity of everything from dirt to the mash tank. It will continue to wreak its devastation as long as we continue to buy and eat its products and elect lawmakers who take corporate donations in lieu of curbing corporate excess. We need to be aware of and responsible for what ends up on our plates and in our beverages. The need for communities to grow more of their own food intelligently and to support local farmers has never been greater.

Yours in health and high spirits,

16 Cocktail

RECIPES

MAI RYE TAI

A sophisticated fruit punch

Ingredients

1 large holy basil blossom

4 drops Lactart (lemon juice can be used as a substitute)

Ice

2½ ounces Copper Fox Rye Whisky

½ Edy's Grape Outshine (frozen) Fruit Bar, melted

½ ounce Rose's Sweetened Lime Juice

½ ounce grapefruit juice

3 ounces raspberry-flavored seltzer water

Pineapple chunk and holy basil leaf for garnish

Tools

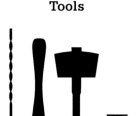

How to Make It

1. Muddle the holy basil blossom and Lactart lightly in a large rocks glass.
2. Crush ice in the Lewis bag with the muddler, and fill ¾ of the glass with crushed ice.
3. Add the rye whisky, melted frozen fruit bar, lime juice, and the grapefruit juice.
4. Stir well.
5. Add the raspberry seltzer water.
6. Garnish with a pineapple chunk and a holy basil leaf.

Aloha!

MASON-DAWSON GIMLET

Minty and fresh with a hint of citrus
and a pop of tangy ginger ale

Ingredients

Mint ice sphere (follow the recipe on page 61, using
fresh Kentucky Colonel mint as the botanical)

2 ounces Wasmund's Rye Spirit

1 ounce Sage-Lemon-Rosemary Syrup (recipe on
page 65)

3½ ounces ginger ale

Kentucky Colonel mint for garnish

Tools

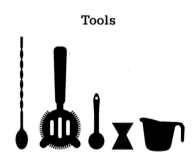

How to Make It

1. Put the ice sphere in a large rocks glass.
2. Add the Rye Spirit and Sage-Lemon-Rosemary Syrup over the ice sphere.
3. Stir.
4. Add the ginger ale.
5. Garnish with a mint leaf.

Here's to you!

BAY SPIRIT

Sittin' on the dock of the bay, watchin' the honey and cucumber mix with the earthy bay leaf to create a big, bold, yet balanced afternoon sippin' drink

Ingredients

2 cucumber chunks

1 tablespoon amber wildflower honey

2 ounces Wasmund's Single Malt Spirit

1 ounce dry vermouth (Dolin)

½ ounce Bay Leaf Jus

Mint-ginger ice sphere (recipe on page 63)

3 ounces club soda with lemon spritz

Thin wheels of lemon and cucumber for garnish

Tools

Bay Leaf Jus

Gently sauté 2 bay leaves in 2 ounces of water until the liquid is reduced by half. Cool to room temperature.

How to Make It

1. Muddle the cucumber with the honey in the bottom of a large rocks glass.
2. Add the Single Malt Spirit, dry vermouth, and Bay Leaf Jus.
3. Add the ice sphere.
4. If you don't want cucumber chunks in your drink, strain them out.
5. Add the club soda. Stir carefully.
6. Garnish with thin lemon and cucumber wheels.

Enjoy!

Ingredients

3 sage leaves

1 teaspoon Lemon Honey Mix

5 ounces VERY ripe honeydew melon

¼ teaspoon chocolate extract (this is essential)

6 ounces lemonade

Ice

2 ounces Wasmund's Single Malt Spirit

1 lime wedge and 1 slice honeydew melon for garnish

Tools

Lemon Honey Mix
Blend 1 tablespoon honey and 1 teaspoon lemon juice

How to Make It

1. Muddle the sage leaves in a tumbler with the Lemon-Honey Mix.
2. Add the muddled mix to a blender. A Vitamix or immersion blender works best. (If using an immersion blender, keep the mix in the tumbler.)
3. Add the melon, chocolate extract, and lemonade to the muddled mix.
4. Blend well.
5. Crush ice in the Lewis bag with the muddler. Fill a margarita glass halfway with crushed ice.
6. Pour the Single Malt Spirit over the ice.
7. Add the blended mix to the glass and stir well.
8. Garnish with a lime wedge and a slice of honeydew melon.

Cin Cin!

PINK & SMITTEN

Fruity and effervescent, with depth

Ingredients

1 ounce vodka

2 ounces Alcyone Tannat Dessert Wine (or a quality ruby port)

3 ounces Le Colture Spumante (or sparkling sake)

Borage and calendula blossoms for garnish

Tools

How to Make It

1. Add the vodka to a champagne flute.
2. Add the dessert wine.
3. Add the spumante.
4. Garnish with borage and calendula blossoms.

Cheerio!

PURPLE HAZE

Berry with a hit of lemon ... the whisky adds
an earthy depth to the magic of orange mint,
lavender, and honey

Ingredients

2 or 3 large, fresh blackberries

¼ cup fresh blueberries

1 tablespoon amber wildflower honey, melted

2 to 3 sprigs of orange mint

2 sprigs of lavender leaves and blossoms

3 or 4 lemon balm ice cubes (follow the recipe on
page 61, using fresh lemon balm as the botanical)

2 ounces Copper Fox Rye Whisky

3 to 4 ounces club soda

Tools

How to Make It

1. Muddle the blackberries, blueberries, melted honey, orange mint, and lavender
    in a large rocks glass.
2. Add the lemon-balm ice cubes.
3. Add the rye whisky and club soda.
4. Mix well.

Here's lookin' at you, kid, ... through the Purple Haze!

LEE LEE FIZZ

Minty with a little sweetness, this is a favorite drink for a warm, sunny day ... or any day that you wish was warm and sunny

Ingredients

Hearty handful of Kentucky Colonel mint leaves

2 ounces Wasmund's Rye Spirit or Stay Tuned PathoGin

Mint-ginger ice sphere (recipe on page 63) (a lemon balm or mint ice sphere can be used as a substitute)

4 ounces ginger ale

Sprig of lavender for garnish

Tools

How to Make It

1. Muddle the mint in a shaker with a little Rye Spirit or gin.
2. Add the muddled mint to a martini glass.
3. Add a mint-ginger ice sphere.
4. Pour the remaining Rye Spirit or gin over the ice sphere.
5. Add the ginger ale.
6. Stir well.
7. Garnish with a sprig of lavender.

Bottoms up!

B-RYE-L-T

This harvest cocktail utilizes good things from your garden to make a sweet and spicy sandwich in a glass!

Ingredients

1 sprig rosemary

2 sage leaves

3 to 5 arugula leaves (depending on their size)

2 ounces fresh heirloom tomato (black variety preferred)

Dash of Worcestershire sauce

Hearty dash of hot sauce (sriracha or Tabasco Pepper Sauce)

Ice

2½ ounces Copper Fox Rye Whisky

1 slice of cooked bacon for garnish

Tools

How to Make It

1. Muddle the rosemary, sage, and arugula along with the heirloom tomato in a large rocks glass. Muddle well to ensure that the herbs are pulverized.
2. Add the Worcestershire sauce, cayenne pepper, and hot sauce.
3. Crush ice in the Lewis bag with the muddler. Fill the glass halfway with crushed ice.
4. Add the rye whisky to the glass.
5. Stir well.
6. Garnish with bacon.

Tchin! Tchin!

PUMPKIN SPICE MANHATTAN

This Thanksgiving cocktail (created by Justin Armstrong) tastes like something that Grandma would have made!

Ingredients

2 ounces Copper Fox Rye Whisky

½ ounce sweet vermouth (Dolin Vermouth de Chambéry Rouge)

1 ounce Torani Pumpkin Spice Syrup

Splash of Disaronno Amaretto

Pumpkin Sugar Rim

Ice

Tools

Pumpkin Sugar Rim

½ cup granulated sugar

1½ teaspoons cinnamon

½ teaspoon powdered ginger

¼ teaspoon nutmeg

Mix these ingredients together.

How to Make It

1. Make the Pumpkin Sugar and set aside.
2. Put a few ice cubes into a large rocks glass.
3. Add the rye whisky, sweet vermouth, Torani syrup, and Amaretto to the glass.
4. Pour the contents of the glass into a tumbler.
5. Using the residual moisture on the glass rim, coat the rim with Pumpkin Sugar.
6. Pour the tumbler contents back into the glass.

Give thanks.

PEPPERMINT KNICKERS

Chocolaty, minty, and whisky! Who could ask for more? ... Okay, just one more.

Ingredients

2 ounces Wasmund's Single Malt Whisky

½ ounce Kahlúa

1½ ounces Peppermint Simple Syrup (recipe on page 64)

Ice

Peppermint ice sphere (recipe on page 64)

Red-and-white dianthus blossom and mint leaves for garnish

Tools

How to Make It

1. Add the whisky, Kahlúa, and Mint Simple Syrup into the shaker with ice.
2. Shake well.
3. Put a peppermint ice sphere into a martini glass.
4. Strain the contents of the shaker over the ice sphere into the glass.
5. Garnish with a red-and-white dianthus blossom and mint leaves.

Cheers!

COJONES

Aromatic cocktail with mellow orange and chocolate flavors with a hint of home-baked spice … Perfect with a cigar

Ingredients

1/8 teaspoon cinnamon

1/8 teaspoon allspice

1 vanilla bean

Ice to fill the shaker

1½ ounces Wasmund's Single Malt Whisky

½ ounce Grand Marnier

¼ ounce chocolate liqueur (such as Godiva)

¼ ounce sweet vermouth (Antica)

2 drops sambuca

Mint leaves for garnish

Tools

How to Make It

1. In a dry sauté pan, toast the cinnamon, allspice, and vanilla bean until they become fragrant.
2. Fill the shaker with ice.
3. Add the toasted spices to the shaker.
4. Add the whisky, Grand Marnier, chocolate liqueur, sweet vermouth, and sambuca to the shaker.
5. Stir. Don't shake.
6. Strain into a cordial glass.
7. Garnish with mint leaves.

Salud!

WHISKY TWIZZLER

Whisky and candy ... yum!

Ingredients

1½ teaspoons fresh sage

1½ teaspoons fresh rosemary

1½ tablespoons melted raw honey

Ice

2 ounces Copper Fox Rye Whisky

1 ounce Chambord liqueur

Soda water to fill the glass

1 Twizzlers Strawberry Twist candy and a rosemary
sprig for garnish

Tools

How to Make It

1. In a large rocks glass, muddle the sage and rosemary with the melted raw honey.
2. Crush the ice in the Lewis bag with the muddler, and fill ¾ of the glass with crushed ice.
3. Add the rye whisky and Chambord to the glass.
4. Add soda water to fill the glass, and stir.
5. Garnish with a Twizzlers Twist and a rosemary sprig.

Prost!

WHISKY-LOVIN' RUSSIAN

Marzipan and a porcupine fur hat
with a cherry on top

Ingredients

4 or 5 cinnamon basil leaves

2 to 4 mint leaves

Espresso-almond ice sphere (recipe on page 66)

2 ounces Copper Fox Rye Whisky or Wasmund's
Single Malt Whisky

½ ounce Disaronno Amaretto

½ ounce light cream

2 maraschino cherries for garnish

Tools

How to Make It

1. Muddle the cinnamon basil and mint leaves in a large rocks glass.
2. Add an espresso-almond ice sphere to the glass.
3. Add the rye whisky and Amaretto. Stir well.
4. Add the cream. Stir well.
5. Garnish with 2 maraschino cherries.

Za zdorov'ye!

RINGIN' RYE

Justin Armstrong's recipe created for New Year's Eve, this is light almond with a little rye funk

Ingredients

1 ounce Wasmund's Rye Spirit

1 ounce Chartreuse (green)

1 ounce Amarguinha (Portuguese almond liqueur)

1 ounce fresh-squeezed lemon juice

1 tablespoon honey (use a light local variety)

Ice

Tools

How to Make It

1. Fill a shaker with ice and add all the ingredients except the garnish.
2. Shake well.
3. Strain into a martini glass.

Happy New Year!

FIRST FENCE

This summer cocktail is fresh and fruity with an herbal kick

Ingredients

½ tablespoon Vietnamese coriander

½ tablespoon Tagetes (Mexican marigold) (fresh tarragon can be used as a substitute)

¼ cup loosely packed raspberries, strawberries, or watermelon chunks

1 tablespoon fresh apple mint

Ice

2 ounces Copper Fox Rye Whisky

½ ounce Grand Marnier

Dash of orange bitters (Peychaud's Aromatic Cocktail Bitters can be used as a substitute)

Orange wheel, mint leaves, and a Tagetes blossom for garnish

Tools

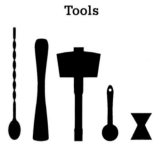

How to Make It

1. Muddle the Vietnamese coriander and Tagetes with a splash of rye whisky in a large rocks glass.
2. If using raspberries or strawberries, rinse them and allow to drain.
3. Muddle the raspberries, strawberries, or watermelon chunks with the apple mint in the glass.
4. Crush the ice in the Lewis bag with the muddler, and fill ¾ of the glass with crushed ice.
5. Add the rye whisky, Grand Marnier, and bitters.
6. Stir well.
7. Garnish with an orange wheel, mint leaves, and a Tagetes blossom.

À votre santé!

HOLY SPIRIT

Tasty, with floral and licorice notes,
this drink will stir your spirit

Ingredients

3-inch piece of fresh angelica stem

1 tablespoon of holy basil

A few sprigs of lavender blossoms

2 ounces Wasmund's Rye Spirit

½ ounce absinthe

Juniper-infused ice sphere (recipe on page 62)

3 ounces ginger ale

A sprig of lavender blossoms for garnish

Tools

How to Make It

1. Muddle the angelica stem, holy basil, and lavender blossoms in a shaker.
2. Add the Rye Spirit and absinthe, and stir well.
3. Add a juniper-infused ice sphere to a martini glass.
4. Strain the contents of the shaker over the ice sphere into the glass.
5. Add the ginger ale.
6. Garnish with a sprig of lavender blossoms.

May the spirit be with you!

HERB-INFUSED SIMPLE SYRUP FOR USE AS COCKTAIL ICE

Ingredients

Use a 2:1 ratio of sugar to water—that is, 2 parts sugar to 1 part water. Add ¼ part botanicals (unless the recipe calls for a different amount). Use only leaves and blooms. Stems can add bitterness.

A basic recipe might be 4 cups of sugar, 2 cups of water, and ½ cup of herbs, but you can make cocktail ice in greater or smaller quantities.

How to Make It

1. Bring the water to a boil.
2. Pour the sugar into the boiling water, stirring constantly until the sugar is completely dissolved.
3. Remove the mixture from the heat.
4. Add the botanicals to the sugar water mixture. Let them steep for 1 to 2 hours. The resulting solution will be the liquid for your ice. It should be potent.
5. Strain and filter the mixture. (You can use a coffee filter to catch the "dust.")
6. Decant the liquid mixture into ice sphere molds or ice cube trays.
7. Label and freeze.

JUNIPER-INFUSED ICE SPHERES

Ingredients

2 cups sugar

1 cup water

1 teaspoon juniper berries

How to Make It

1. Bring the water to a boil.
2. Pour the sugar into the boiling water, stirring constantly until the sugar is completely dissolved.
3. Remove the mixture from the heat.
4. Add the juniper berries to the sugar water mixture. Let them steep for 1 to 2 hours.
5. Do not strain.
6. Decant the liquid into ice sphere molds or the desired shape ice tray. Make sure there is at least one juniper berry in each ice sphere or ice cube.
7. Label and freeze.

MINT-GINGER ICE SPHERES

Ingredients

2 cups sugar

1 cup water

3 tablespoons fresh chopped ginger

½ cup of mint leaves

How to Make It

1. Bring the water to a boil.
2. Pour the sugar into the boiling water, stirring constantly until the sugar is completely dissolved.
3. Remove the mixture from the heat.
4. Add the ginger and mint to the sugar water mixture. Let them steep for 1 to 2 hours.
5. Strain and filter the mixture.
6. Decant the liquid into ice sphere molds or the desired shape ice tray.
7. Label and freeze.

PEPPERMINT SIMPLE SYRUP/ICE SPHERES

Ingredients

2 cups sugar

1 cup water

½ cup of peppermint leaves

Peppermint Starlight hard candies (for ice spheres)

How to Make It

1. Bring the water to a boil.
2. Pour the sugar into the boiling water, stirring constantly until the sugar is completely dissolved.
3. Remove the mixture from the heat.
4. Add the peppermint to the sugar water mixture. Let steep for 1 to 2 hours.
5. Strain and filter the mixture.
6. Reserve a portion (1½ ounces for each cocktail) of the Peppermint Simple Syrup for use in the Peppermint Knickers cocktails.
7. Decant the remainder of the syrup into ice sphere molds (or the desired shape ice tray).
8. Add a Peppermint Starlight hard candy to each ice sphere mold.
9. Label and freeze.

SAGE-LEMON-ROSEMARY SYRUP

Ingredients

1 cup sugar

½ cup water

1 teaspoon lemon peel

3 sage leaves

2 sprigs of rosemary

How to Make It

1. Bring the water to a boil.
2. Pour the sugar into the boiling water, stirring constantly until the sugar is completely dissolved.
3. Remove the mixture from the heat.
4. Add the lemon peel, sage, and rosemary to the sugar water mixture. Let them steep for 1 to 2 hours.
5. Strain the mixture.

ESPRESSO-ALMOND ICE SPHERES

Ingredients

Espresso

2 drop almond extract

How to Make It

1. Prepare 2 to 3 ounces of espresso. (Strong instant coffee can be used as a substitute.)
2. Add 2 drops almond extract and stir.
3. Add water to barely cover the bottom of each ice sphere mold. (If using instant coffee, do not add water to the mold.)
4. Decant the espresso-almond mixture into ice sphere molds or the desired shape ice tray.
5. Label and freeze.

NOTES

NOTES

NOTES

NOTES

REFERENCES

[1]Joseph Mercola, "Getting to the Root of How GMO Plants Harm Food Production and Your Health," Mercola.com (May 19, 2013),
http://articles.mercola.com/sites/articles/archive/2013/05/19/gmo-harms-food-production.aspx.

[2] J.G. Davis and D. Whiting, "Choosing a Soil Amendment," Colorado State University Extension, Fact Sheet No. 7.235 (updated April 19, 2013), http://www.ext.colostate.edu/ pubs/garden/07235.html.

[3] Davis and Whiting, "Choosing a Soil Amendment."

[4] Ben Watson, "Hybrid or Open Pollinated," National Gardening Association, p. 3,
http:// www.garden.org/subchannels/care/seeds?q=show&id=293.

[5] Watson, "Hybrid or Open Pollinated," p. 4.

[6] Mercola, "Getting to the Root of How GMO Plants Harm Food Production and Your Health."

[7] Institute of Science in Society Special Report: "Why Glyphosate Should Be Banned," October 10, 2012,
http://www.i-sis.org.uk/Why_Glyphosate_Should_be_Banned.php.

[8] Mercola, "Getting to the Root of How GMO Plants Harm Food Production and Your Health."

[9] Joseph Mercola, "Toxicology Expert Speaks Out About Roundup and GMOs," Mercola.com (October 6, 2013),
http://articles.mercola.com/sites/articles/archive/2013/10/06/dr-huber-gmo-foods.aspx.

[10] Mercola, "Toxicology Expert Speaks Out About Roundup and GMOs."

IN THE DIRT AT MY PLACE

This is a cultivar list with notes on findings, failures, and successes from the summers of 2011 and 2012.

Phase 1: Prep

A year before I decided to start the "little big garden," I grew at least six different varieties of sunflowers as a soil remediate in the spot I'd reserved for the garden. The following winter, I grew hairy vetch, rye, wheat, and fodder radish, which I turned under the soil to use as green manure in the spring. Growing cover crops instead of leaving the ground fallow in the off-season is a phenomenal way to accomplish two important results at once. First, it creates greater capacity for improved soil biology by adding humic matter to the dirt when you recycle those plants into your dirt. Their decomposition is critical for fostering microbial populations. Second is the satisfaction of participating in the growing process in the winter. In areas with short and unpredictable growing seasons, growing plants all year long is a happy thing. In the midst of dreary winter, I never cease to get a kick out of seeing the silly, green, sprouted head of a seed, sown by my hand, emerging from the dirt and snow.

Phase 2: Planting
Herbs/Edible Flowers

These are the herbs and edible flowers I planted. Most are easy to grow. All are delicious. Annual plants are designated with an asterisk (*).

Angelica
Arugula
Basils *
> Holy (A heavy seeder, with a unique, bubble-gum-like flavor)
> Cinnamon (Large, with a lovely fragrance and blooms)
> Lemon (Delightful citrus flavor, pretty blooms)
> Genovese (Traditional, outstanding flavor)

Bergamot
Borage
Calendula
Chamomile
Chives (The blossoms are amazing! Makes great flavored butter.)
Cilantro
Dianthus
French tarragon (Overwintered in our hoop house, and did great.)
Lavender
Lemon balm
Lemon grass *
Mints (Essential for cocktails)
        Kentucky Colonel
        Orange
        Spearmint
        Peppermint
        Apple
Nasturtium*
Rosemary
Sage
Shungiku chrysanthemum (Has really pretty flowers. The petals have the best flavor, as the centers are bitter.
        The greens can be harvested when the plant is 5-6 inches tall.)
Tagetes Mexican marigold *
Thymes
        Lemon
        French
Vietnamese coriander *

Vegetables

These are the vegetables I grew. All were started from seed.

Broccoli (Direct-sown seeds did better than transplants. However, cabbage loopers—those cutesy little white
        butterflies—did some damage, then the heat, and then the drought. No harvest.)
        Purple Peacock
        Romanesco

Copenhagen Market Cabbage (Met the same plight as the broccoli with cabbage loopers. Applied diatomaceous earth and it helped somewhat. I harvested enough to make some outstanding Haluski. It's a Pittsburgh thing.)

Eggplant mix (Whites and purples—beautiful harvest)

Lettuces, heirloom varieties (Did very well growing under and among the tomatoes, chives, and nasturtiums. Survived the heat.)

Melons (Direct sown, they produced fruit but ultimately succumbed to wilt. I do not have ideal soil conditions.)
- Charentais
- Haogen

Mizuna greens (Did well early, but as the temperatures rose, the Mizuna died.)

Parsley, Broad Leafed Plain (Did great. Prefers partial shade.)

Snow Peas, Oregon Sugar Pod (Produced very well for 2 months despite unfavorable temperatures. Transplanted well. Has the best root mass of all cultivars.)

Peppers
- Hot pepper mix (Produced lots of peppers despite the drought. Delightfully hot.)
- Jimmy Nardello's Sweet Italian Frying Pepper (Healthy production. Not large plants.)
- Purple bell peppers (Stunted growth but produced better as the season went on. Lovely flavor.)

Tomatoes (I had 10 plants of each variety—way too many.)
- Green Zebra
- Black from Tula
- Old German
- Stupice
- Roma
- Paul Robison
- Purple Cherokee
- Peacevine cherry
- Plus about a half dozen of various cherry volunteers from last year

Dragon Langerie Wax Beans (Not so successful but produced some surprisingly cool beans.)

GUIDE TO RESOURCES

Sources for Gardening Products and Information

Advancing Eco-Agriculture
4551 Parks West Road
Middlefield, Ohio 44062
800-495-6603
www.growbetterfood.com

Bountiful Gardens
1712-D South Main Street
Willits, California 95490
707-459-6410
www.bountifulgardens.org

Ecology Action
5798 Ridgewood Road
Willits, California 95490
707-459-0150
www.growbiointensive.org/index.html

The Growers Exchange
11110 Sandy Fields Road
Richmond, VA 23030
1-888-829-6201
http://www.thegrowers-exchange.com

International Ag Labs
800 W. Lake Avenue
PO Box 788
Fairmont, Minnesota 56031
507-235-6909
www.aglabs.com

The Josephine Porter Institute for Applied Bio-Dynamics, Inc.
201 East Main Street, Suite 14
Floyd, Virginia 24091
540-745-7030
www.jpibiodynamics.org

Peaceful Valley Farm & Garden Supply
PO Box 2209
125 Clydesdale Court
Grass Valley, California 95945
888-784-1722
www.groworganic.com

Pike Agri-Lab Supplies, Inc.
154 Claybrook Road
PO Box 67
Jay, Maine 04239
207-897-9267
866-745-3247 (Toll free)
www.pikeagri.com

Enlightening Reading

Carole Ann Rollins and Elaine Ingham. *10 Steps to Gardening with Nature*. Novato, CA: Nature Technologies International, 2011.

Michael Pollan. *The Botany of Desire: A Plant's-Eye View of the World*. New York: Random House Trade Paperbacks, 2001.

Jessica Walliser. *Good Bug Bad Bug: Who's Who, What They Do, and How to Manage Them Organically*. Pittsburgh, PA: St. Lynn's Press, 2008.

Jeffrey M. Smith. *Genetic Roulette: The Documented Health Risks of Genetically Engineered Foods*. Yes! Books, 2007.

Enlightening Viewing

Genetic Roulette: The Gamble of Our Lives—A documentary film (2012) that explores the issues surrounding genetically modified foods and how they affect our health.

Mondovino—A documentary film (2004) about the impact of globalization on the world's different wine regions.

Numen: The Nature of Plants—A documentary film (2009) focusing on the healing power of plants and the natural world.

ACKNOWLEDGMENTS

First I want to thank Justin Armstrong, a dear friend and fellow admirer of all things Vermont. He was an indispensable help with the recipes and has kept me going in somewhat of a straight line in writing this book. Not an easy task.

I also want to acknowledge the people at Copper Fox Distillery, makers of Copper Fox Rye Whisky and Wasmund's Single Malt Whisky and mentors of Stay Tuned Distillery. From you, I have learned from the best.

Many thanks to the following people for their expertise in making this book a reality and for their overall fabulous-ness:

Editor: Deborah Gouge of Seeds Green Printing and Design
Layout/Design: Camden Leeds of Seeds Green Printing and Design
Printer: Jeff Shaw of Seeds Green Printing and Design
Photographer: Adam Milliron
Jason Boone: For sharing a damned good bottle of whisky

ABOUT THE AUTHOR

Lee Ann Sommerfeld is a classically trained musician who lives in Pittsburgh, Pennsylvania, where she is co-owner of Stay Tuned Distillery, a craft distillery dedicated to small-batch, seasonally relevant gins and Pennsylvania's home to Copper Fox Whisky. Her jobs are self-described as "chief, cook, and bottle washer." She supplements the botanicals for Stay Tuned gins from her gardens.

Her urban gardening pursuits took root a few years ago. As a participant in a garden group whose aim was to grow high brix tomatoes, she discovered that nutrition and food quality begin in the dirt. After attending a soil biology conference on an Amish farm in Ohio, where speakers and farmers from all over the world shared their knowledge of and frustration with corporate farming practices, she began to understand the impact of industrial agriculture and how polluted our mass food supply is. She now sees the typical supermarket as something closer to a legal chemical-weapons dispensary than a purveyor of nutritious food.

Lee Ann is an active member of Food Democracy Now and serves as the wine chair for Crushed Grapes, an annual charity event that raises money and awareness for Sisters Place, a Pittsburgh-based nonprofit that provides services for single-parent homeless families. She is also a strong advocate for hemp cultivation and medical marijuana legalization. She has been known to shout from street corners and mountaintops "Grow your own and share!"